Wild Creatures
of The World

Written and Illustrated by Tom Romano

Published by AB Film Publishing, Inc.

290 West 12th Street, Suite A
New York, New York 10014
Phone: (212) 741-1441

ISBN: 978-0-9904852-0-9

AB Film Publishing is a consortium of artists and writers, producing
quality literary material

Dedication

This book is dedicated to the memory of Opal Whiteley, a great naturalist with a fire and passion in her heart, and my friend Steve Williamson, Opal's historian. May the love Opal brought to the natural world forever live in our hearts.

Table of Contents

Part 1: Felines of the World

Part 2: Animals of the Northern Areas

PART 1

FELINES
of The World

SOME FELINE SPECIES OF THE WORLD

Species Name	Food Source	Country
Bobcat	Deer, rabbits	United States, Canada
Bengal Tiger	Wild Boars, monkeys	India
Canadian Lynx	Deer, snowshoe hares	United States, Canada
Cougar	Deer, sheep, rabbits	United States, Canada
Snow Leopard	Hares, mice, Ibex, birds	Tibet, Mongolia, Russia
African Lion	Wildebeest, zebra	S. Africa, Senegal, Kenya
African Leopard	Gazelle, impala	S. Africa, Senegal, Kenya
Cheetah	Gazelle, impala, deer	S. Africa, Iran, Senegal
Ocelot	Deer, birds	Colombia, Brazil, Bolivia
Clouded Leopard	goats, pigs, birds, snakes	China, Southeast Asia
Housecat	Cat food, but a mouse or bird will also do	With any cat lover

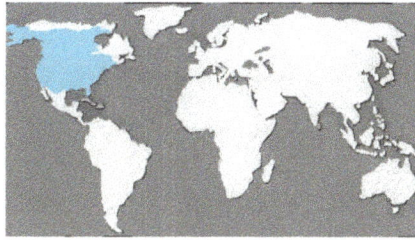

BOBCAT *Lynx rufus*

The bobcat is a smaller cousin to the American lynx. Its dappled coat can blend perfectly in the forest. It lives all over the United States, its food rabbits, mice, and small deer.

Once a bobcat and a bald eagle fought over a fresh kill. It turned out that greed or need dominated all: the eagle was killed outright, and the bobcat died of of the eagle's talon-inflicted wounds later.

The bobcat may wander 25-50 miles, but usually only ventures two or three miles from its territory. The female bobcat is territorial, staking out a home range that varies from two to more than forty square miles, with overlapping of female boundaries uncommon. She marks her territory with urine. Male territories frequently overlap those of other males.

Bobcat kittens are born blind and weigh less than a pound. They are entirely dependent on their mother for food and protection. At nine months of age, however, they leave their mother's protection to establish territories of their own.

Bobcats are common in North American forests. Sometimes, from a distance, they get mistaken for housecats, but the tufted ears and face soon tell the observer their mistake.

BOBCAT

8

BENGAL TIGER

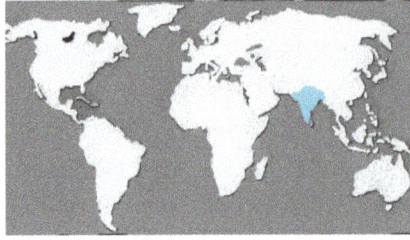

BENGAL TIGER *Panthera tigris tigris*

The biggest cat on earth is the Siberian tiger. It lives in the forests of Russia. It is a huge animal, weighing in at eight hundred pounds, and can kill a wild boar, which it hunts frequently. The animal illustrated here is its smaller cousin, the Bengal tiger. It is found in India and Pakistan, but poaching and hunting have greatly reduced its numbers. There are still a few hundred protected tigers in India's Gir Forest. But even if the animal is protected, there are no guarantees of its safety. Tiger parts are frequently sold on the black market where they fetch high prices, so hunters are willing to take the gamble of illegally killing one. In the highly populous countries of India and Pakistan, there are a lot of desperate, poor people.

Occasionally, the Bengal tiger turns maneater, but these are generally older animals who may raid nearby villages, and get a taste for the flesh of farm animals. From there, things can lead to a quick confrontation with man. The tiger eventually becomes the loser. A tiger may be big and formidable, but he is not going to be a match for a gun.

A former "sport" in India was hunting tigers from the backs of elephants. The elephants would flush the tigers out, and they would be shot by the hunter, quite an unfair advantage.

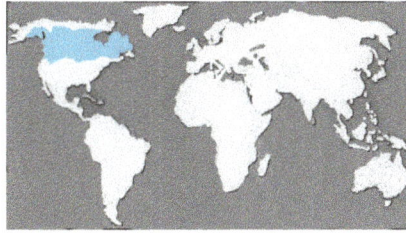

CANADIAN LYNX *Lynx canadensis*

There are a few species of lynx found the world over. The Spanish lynx and Eurasian lynx are two examples of Old World lynxes. The species pictured here is the Canadian gray lynx, the world's largest. Its large, padded feet give it the advantage of surprise in ambushing its prey; it can walk almost noiselessly on deep snow. No wonder some people call this beautiful, elusive animal the ghost of the northern forest.

One of the gray lynx's favorite prey animals is the snowshoe hare. The lynx also hunts deer. It will eat carrion, meadow voles, and even birds. Undoubtedly, this is an animal that has well adjusted itself to surviving in the wild. Creeping silently up on its prey, it quickly ambushes its quarry, seizing it with its sharp, retractable claws and kills it, usually with a bite to the neck.

The lynx has large eyes and ears and depends on its acute eyesight and hearing for hunting as well as keeping out of danger.

The Spanish lynx of Spain and Portugal is the most critically endangered species of cat on the planet. Only about 200 animals remain. Poaching, poisoning of animals by farmers and trapping have decimated their numbers as recently as the end of the twentieth century. Spanish conservation programs are helping its numbers to increase.

CANADIAN LYNX

MOUNTAIN LION *Puma concolor*

The mountain lion is known by several names, catamount, painter, cougar. The name once struck fear in the hearts of sheepherders and goat farmers, as well as pioneer families.

Besides the predations of wolves, attacks on livestock, especially in the high pastures, meant mountain lions. Usually, however, lions feed on deer, with an occasional jackrabbit as a dietary supplement, or even an occasional bird.

The mountain lion is usually wary of human activities, and generally avoids man. They are sleek, muscular animals, occasionally reaching the weight of over two hundred pounds. Adults are colored a *tawny* color (tan) to darker brown. Occasionally, however, when there is an overpopulation, older, dominant males will literally drive younger males out of their territory. These youngsters are forced to find other areas to claim, and that can spell trouble; their wanderings may bring them to areas of forest near urban sites, and confrontations with man and his dogs. Reports of mountain lion attacks on dogs and cats are rare, but have been documented.

Police have been called in to shoot troublesome cougars in the suburbs. That has triggered controversy between law enforcement officials, conservationists, and homeowners. One argument has been that the cougars should be tranquilized, not shot. The opposing side may maintain that the cougars are too dangerous to have around homes and should be eliminated, as they may also target children.

Deer are overpopulated in many parks today, and their presence has often attracted cougars. If a person encounters a cougar, they are advised to use direct eye contact; a cougar will look away. The person must not run: that will invite a cougar to attack. Standing one's ground might also discourage a mountain lion from attacking.

SNOW LEOPARD

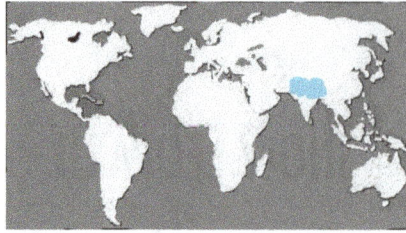

SNOW LEOPARD *Uncia uncia*

Whether in pursuit of an ibex or blending with the snows in the Himalayan mountains, the snow leopard is one of the most elusive of the big cats. Prized for its beautiful fur, the solitary nature and forbidding environment of the snow leopard has helped ensure its survival.

Watching the snow leopard chase an ibex is a spectacle of incredible beauty. One would think that the ibex, because of its speed and ability to run quickly down forty-five degree slopes, would have no predator capable of matching its speed and agility. In a nature program on National Geographic, a snow leopard chasing an ibex equaled its speed and surefootedness leap for leap. The ibex saved itself only by jumping into an icy alpine lake and swimming away, leaving a very frustrated snow leopard.

The total population of snow leopards is roughly estimated at 4,080-6,590 animals, but this figure may be out of date. The actual number of them may be fewer than 2,500 animals.

The snow leopard shows many adaptive traits which help it to survive in its cold mountain environment. Their bodies are stocky, and their fur thickly insulated against the unforgiving high altitude weather.

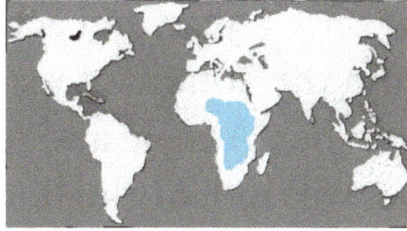

AFRICAN LION *Pantheria leo*

The familiar sight of a *pride* (group) of lions resting in the shade of an acacia tree on the African *bushveldt* (plain) is a part of many television nature programs. The pride is a family unit, usually run by one or two dominant males, often brothers. It is their job to protect the others in the pride from the raids of enemies and fight off other lions trying to take over pride ownership. Within the pride framework, the hunting is done by the females.

A group of lionesses will walk in step with purpose as they gather for the evening hunt. A herd of wildebeest or zebra are the usual prey targets. The lionesses select an animal and creep towards it, working as a team. One lioness will drive the animal towards the female lions lying concealed in the grass, who will then ambush the animal and hopefully bring it down. Death for the hapless zebra or wildebeest can be long and agonizing, usually from not being able to breathe due to one lioness fastening her teeth around its throat, or shock and loss of blood from the other lionesses tearing it apart.

When the prey is subdued, the pride crouches down to eat. Males get the largest portions, with the lionesses then getting their share. Squabbles are common, with animals swatting angrily at each other. The last to be fed are the cubs, and if the prey is consumed by the adults, the youngsters go without. In lean times this has led to more than one cub starving to death.

Females come into heat once a year, and actively *solicit*, or attempt to interest, attention from the dominant males. Playfully she runs from him, and he pursues her. A male and female will mate several times a day. The lion will mount the lioness, holding her neck in his teeth. If he is too slow to dismount, the female may turn and swat at him.

Sometimes in the African wild, predators fight predators. The result can be bloody confrontations between those that seek territorial domination. On the African bushveldt, fights between hyenas and lions can turn deadly, with several animals on both sides severely injured or killed.

AFRICAN LION

LEOPARD

20

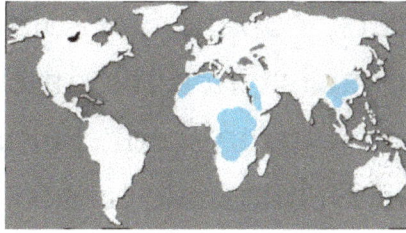

AFRICAN LEOPARD *Panthera pardus*

Leopards are powerful animals. They have elegant, long bodies, large paws, and long tails. Most leopards have yellowish bodies with dark spots. Their neck muscles are very strong, which allows them to drag prey heavier than themselves up a tree and lodge it in the branches. This they do to avoid having their precious food stolen by hyenas or lions. There has been more than once instance of a group of hyenas harassing a leopard up into a tree and stealing its prey before the leopard was able to safely secure it up in the branches.

There have been a few cases when leopards have turned maneater, but that is only with older animals, who can't hunt their natural prey as easily.

Leopards live in *habitats* where they find concealment to stalk their prey. What is a habitat? It's the environment the animal lives in. This can range from the African jungles to along the North African coast to the Arabian peninsula and the Middle East. They also live in the jungles and tropical rainforests of Southeast Asia.

Like many of the big cats, leopards are solitary. They only come together with other leopards when it's time to mate. Leopards mark their territories with urine scent. Females exclude other females in their territories, but male territories will overlap those of females.

A leopard's food source is varied, and may depend on what habitat the animal is found in. In the jungle this would include monkeys (if the leopard can catch them), wild boar, and pea fowl. In the Kalahari desert, however, their food items might include hares, warthogs, and jackals.

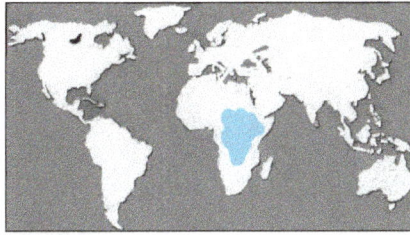

CHEETAH *Acinonyx jubatus*

The fastest animal in the world is the cheetah. A cheetah can go from 0 to 60 miles an hour in a matter of seconds. There are some birds, for example the peregrine falcon, that can fly faster, but no animal can catch the cheetah. The lion and leopard may depend on stealth and ambush to capture fleet-footed prey, but the cheetah can chase it down. It can catch and kill swift animals like the impala and gazelle.

Being slender is both a disadvantage and advantage of being a cheetah. It has great speed, but it's not as physically powerful as a lion, leopard, or even a hyena. It often has to give way when a stronger predator appears and wants to steal the cheetah's prey.

Ranchers in areas near cheetah habitat have found the animals are shy and timid and will not attack livestock when there are dogs and even donkeys around. Cheetahs would rather avoid a fight when necessary since they are not physically strong. Any injury to their bodies might inhibit their ability to run, hence starvation; their speed is their salvation for being able to catch their food.

The Cheetah is not a long distance runner like the horse; it's body is designed to run the short sprint. Because its body does not have temperature regulators, it tends to overheat quickly and must soon stop. When it rests, the cheetah's body temperature lowers.

23

CHEETAH

OCELOT *Leopardus pardalis*

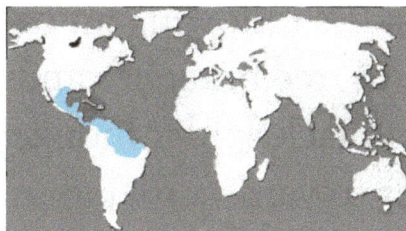

The ocelot is an exotic species of the tropical rainforests. It is a smaller member of the cat family. It's prey can be quite varied from rabbits, mice, and birds, to snakes, lizards, and frogs. It is a strong swimmer, and will even go into the water in search of fish. Like many of the cat family members, or *felines*, it is a solitary animal, but occasionally will hunt with another ocelot.

Ocelots vary in color from light yellow to reddish gray. Sometimes the ocelot gets compared to the margay because both cats live in tropical rainforest. The ocelot is three times the size of the margay, however. It also hunts on the ground, whereas the margay hunts in the branches of trees. Ocelots don't like open space. They prefer the dense cover of the southern forests and brush areas. With clearing and deforestation, the ocelot is now considered an endangered species in the United States. Recent sightings of ocelots have been in some of the southern states, particularly Texas.

The ocelot preys on mammals such as opossum, deer, and anteaters. However, these food items also change from habitat to habitat. On broader plains, the ocelot may feed on iguanas. For instance, in Venezuela, it preys on the spiny-tailed iguana. Spiny pocket mice are also a favorite. In a Peruvian tropical rainforest the ocelot hunts rodents. A number of snakes and birds are also prey.

The ocelot can be a victim of *mobbing*; several animals, all prey, will surround an ocelot and harass it. An observer once noticed a troop of howler monkeys following an ocelot (on the ground) from the safe distance of tree branches and verbally issuing warnings. Another troop of black spider monkeys were observed behaving in a similar manner towards a roving male ocelot.

Ocelots themselves may fall prey to larger predators. A large male ocelot was seen being carried by a jaguar; when the jaguar saw the humans, it dropped its prey and fled.

CLOUDED LEOPARD *Neofelis nebulosa*

The clouded leopard is a feline of tropical forests in Bangladesh, India, Pakistan, Malaysia, and Indochina. Typically, the color of its fur is ochre to dark gray.

The clouded leopard prefers open or closed forest habitat. (forests with open spaces, or tightly packed trees). They were believed to be extinct in Nepal, but in India have been recorded up to an altitude of 1, 450 feet.

The clouded leopard's claws are so sharp it can actually hang upside down and climb head first from tree branches. It is equally at home in both trees and on the ground. It's canines in proportion to its body weight (the leopards average weight is about 28 pounds) are the longest of all the big cats. It's limbs are short, its body stocky, and its paws broad. This also makes it good at creeping through thick forest.

The clouded leopard eats deer, pigs, monkeys, cattle, goats, and birds. Its activities have occasionally put it into conflict with man. Deforestation, habitat destruction, and poaching are most of the reasons why the big cat's numbers are declining. The World Conservation Union has the clouded leopard on its Red List of Threatened Animals. The animal's survival differs in various habitats; in some it is only mildly threatened, but in others, highly endangered.

The clouded leopard is named after the distinctive 'clouds' on its coat; rich brown to dark gray oval shapes and circles are partially edged in black, with the insides a darker color than the background color of the pelt. The base of the fur is a pale yellow to brown, making the darker cloud-like markings look even more distinctive in appearance.

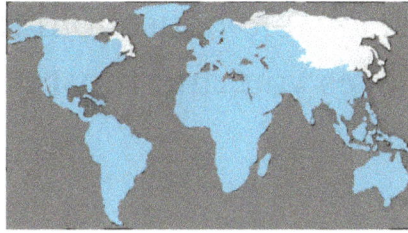

HOUSECAT *Felis catus*

This cat is your curious, lovable household kitty. She loves her home (hopefully) she loves you, and most of all, her meals. (And they'd better be on time).

One would think that cats, because they're often solitary, would not be creatures of habit. But they do, in fact, enjoy favorite spots. It might be a spot where they can look out your window and watch what's going on outside. It might be that old cushion in the corner that looks old and tattered to you, but is a perfect snooze place for your feline. One day, upon returning home, I was surprised to see my kitty lazily stretching himself...on the top of an automobile tire. (And yes, the tire was attached to a car).

Sometimes a housecat will mate with a wildcat, producing a strain of offspring. Housecats, like their wild cousins, are opportunists, taking advantage of food possibilities. Even after a good meal, your kitty may pester you for more, and then not eat it. I had a cat once, who, as soon as she knew I was gazing at her, would automatically head for her dishes. You don't train a cat, I concluded, but they can surely train you.

Occasionally your cat will bring you home a thank offering; if you find a dead mouse or bird by the back door of your house, it's there because they're giving it to you out of love for having a good home.

PART 2

Creatures
of the Northern Areas

SOME ARCTIC ANIMALS

Species Name	Food Source	Where lives
Gray Fox	Eggs, insects, berries, mice	U.S., Mexico
Musk Ox	Grasses, reeds, sedges	Canada, Alaska
Caribou	Lichens, mosses	Canada, Alaska
Timber Wolf	Deer, elk, caribou	U.S., Canada
Kodiak Bear	Moose, deer, berries, fish	Kodiak Island, Alaska
Grizzly Bear	Deer, elk, grubs, fish, honey	U.S., Canada, Alaska
Lemming	Plants, roots, grasses	North America, Asia
Wolverine	Caribou, rodents, plants	U.S., Canada, Alaska, Eurasia
Polar Bear	Seals	U.S., Canada, Norway, Sweden
Fur Seal	Fish, birds, squid	Antarctica
Northern Right Whale	Small fish, krill	North Atlantic Ocean
Walrus	Crabs, various mollusks	Arctic, N. Atlan., Pacific Oceans
Killer Whale (Orca)	Seals, Porpoises, fish	All oceans
Snowy Owl	Hares, fish, mice, rats	Canada, Alaska, Greenland
Chinook Salmon	Herring, anchovy	Pacific Ocean

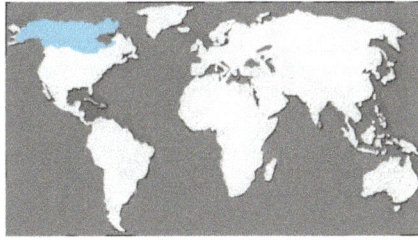

ARCTIC FOX *Vulpes lagopus*

This arctic fox has chosen a nice spot for a nap. He looks very relaxed, don't you think? Arctic foxes are a distinct species from red foxes, gray foxes, and silver foxes. In summer, the arctic fox's coat turns a brownish gray. In winter, however, the arctic fox's coat is pure white, so he can hide in the snow. That makes it easier to creep on his prey, which may be mice or snowshoe hares.

MUSK OX *Ovibos moschatus*

This is the musk ox. They like to pair up or roam in herds. In the far north it is also an animal that has learned that survival depends on force of numbers. Often, when there is an enemy, the musk oxen will form an impenetrable circle around their calves. Most predators, even a pack of wolves or a grizzly bear, might hesitate to cross an angry musk ox and his sharp horns.

The musk ox is a survivor of the Ice Age. It has evolved a thick coat which allows it to survive in its harsh winter environment. And its fierce nature affords it protection against predators.

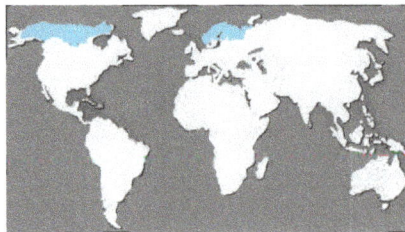

CARIBOU *Rangifer tarandus*

The caribou can be called the workhorse of the arctic. Some cultures, such as the Laplanders of the far north, herd caribou, known as reindeer. They depend on the caribou for meat, clothing, and transportation. These are the same animals that pull Santa Claus's sleigh. The caribou has been *domesticated*, or tamed, by the Laplanders for hundreds, thousands of years.

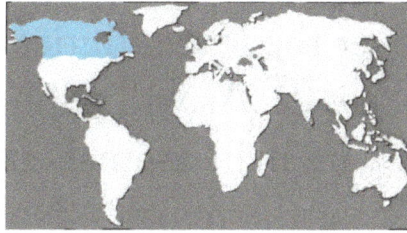

TIMBER WOLF *Canis lupus americanus*

The northern gray wolf is also called the timber wolf. It runs in packs, usually led by an *alpha*, or dominant male. Usually wolf-packs have a dominant male, and a dominant female, called the alpha female. There is a strict hierarchy in any wolf pack of dominant and subordinate animals. The second-in-command male and female in a wolfpack are called the *beta male* and *beta female.*

The beta wolves take over the leader duties if something happens to the alpha male and female. As with alpha wolves, the beta male keeps the subordinate male animals strictly in line, while his mate does the same for the females. Not surprisingly, the alpha male and female are mates, as are the beta male and female. The strict rules of dominance and subordination are honored at all times, and enforced by the dominant animal, regardless of whether the animals are alpha or beta.

Once upon a time, wolves were found in nearly all fifty lower states. During the nineteenth century, thousands of wolves were killed. Wolves have been reintroduced in some states to their former range, such as Yellowstone National Park. Other places, like Isle Royale in Minnesota, have a population of gray wolves who immigrated from Canada. Rumours of wolf sightings, however, continue to surface in other states, such as California and Oregon. It is thought, for example, that in remote areas of the Sierra Nevada range, there might even be a wolfpack or two.

Wolves generally mate for life. The sound of a wolfpack howling in the mountains or forest is unforgettable. It was terrifying for the pioneers and early settlers; they always had guns at the ready to protect themselves. Early travelers passing through the mountains talked of how the wolves would each take a different pitch when they would howl; this sound was particularly frightening. But the wolves may have only been communicating their solidarity and community through a pack howling session.

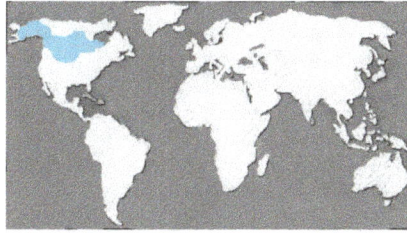

GRIZZLY BEAR *Ursus arctus horribilis*

This is the Kodiak, or Alaskan brown bear. He is a giant cousin of the North American grizzly bear. Only a few hundred of these powerful predators survive on Kodiak Island off the mainland shore of Alaska. Alaska remains the last true stronghold for brown bears worldwide. There are huge areas of wilderness that are perfect for these bears to roam.

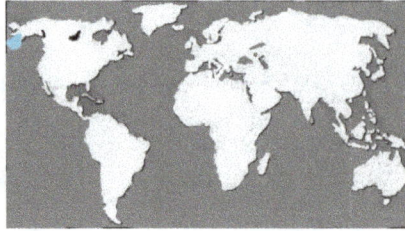

KODIAK BEAR *Ursus arctus middendorffi*

Size distinction:
man and the Kodiak bear

Scientists at one time classified the grizzly and brown bears as separate species. Today, they are thought to be the same species, although the Kodiak brown bears are called a *subspecies* or variation, of the grizzly. How does one differentiate the brown bear from the black bear? The brown bear has a distinct "hump" on its shoulder, and longer, straighter claws than the black.

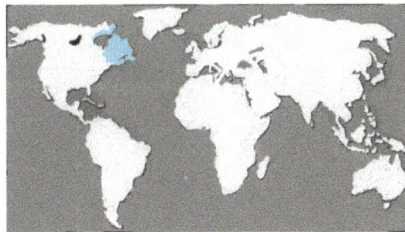

LEMMING *Dicrostonyx torquatus*

The lemming has a strange story. Each year thousands of these animals migrate. Many are killed just by being trampled. Then they reach the ocean, and without a thought, plunge into the icy waters, struggling to reach land beyond the sea. Soon the water is full of hundreds of these animals, struggling to swim. Many don't complete the journey, slipping beneath the waves and drowning.

WOLVERINE *Gulo gulo*

Wolverines are ferocious animals. In the nineteenth century, their pelts made them desirable, but to a fur trapper the last animal he wanted to face in his traps was a snarling wolverine. There is even a report of a wolverine killing a black bear. The bear made the mistake of trying to crush the wolverine in its paws. The wolverine sliced into the bear's chest cavity and literally, tore out its heart. The bear fell dead, and the wolverine, covered with the bear's blood, casually trotted off.

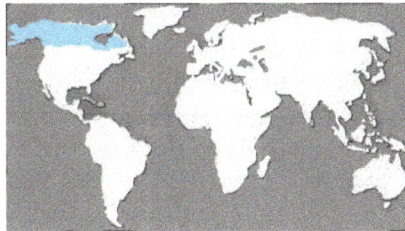

POLAR BEAR *Ursus maritimus*

This polar bear is taking an icy dip in the ocean. He doesn't seem to mind the cold a bit. A polar bear has a thick layer of *blubber* (fat) under his skin that, along with densely packed fur, provides all the insulation from the cold he'll need.

A polar bear's favorite food is seals. A bear will find a hole in the ice where seals come up to breathe, and wait patiently. When he sees the air bubbles of a surfacing seal, he'll wait until he has a good chance of grabbing it. Sometimes he'll even strike the ice with his forepaws repeatedly to break it and get at the seal underneath.

Polar bears will sometimes raid garbage cans in human settlements. Similar to black bears that can become park nuisances, there are some polar bears that, once they get a taste of human food leftovers, will come back again and again to the towns. This can cause major problems; polar bears are exceedingly dangerous, and have been known to turn maneater. It can also happen when the polar bear's natural food is hard to find. When there is a problem bear, a specialist needs to be called in to *tranquilize* the animal. The bears are shot with a special dart (from a gun) which puts them to sleep. Then they are moved to a different location and released.

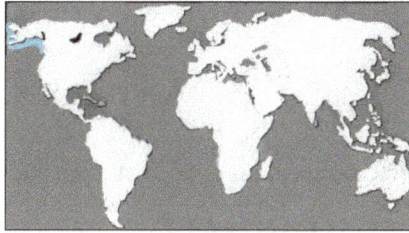

FUR SEAL *Arctocephalus gazella*

The seal below is resting. He's taking some time off from swimming in the sea. He's sitting on top of a rock scanning the ocean for enemies. Hungry sharks may be lurking in the area waiting to snatch an unsuspecting seal. Killer whales may lie offshore in packs ready to pounce. And if the seal needs to come up in the ice to breathe he must beware of polar bears. He may also be watching seabirds such as gulls and terns. If they are circling an area, it might mean a meal of schooling fish.

NORTHERN RIGHT WHALE *Eubalaena glacialis*

The northern right whale got its name because it was considered "unsinkable" by early whalers. After being harpooned, its carcass had a tendency to float rather than sink like other whale species; therefore it was a "right" whale.

The northern right whale can weigh up to 70 tons. It has a stocky body with no dorsal fin. Right whales are *skimmers:* that is, they feed by removing prey from the water with the use of their *baleen.* Baleen is a soft substance in the whale's mouth. The whales will swim through zooplankton with their mouths open; that way, the prey will wash through their baleen. The baleen acts as a kind of sieve through which the food is filtered out of the water. This is completely different from the toothed whales such as the sperm whale, which feeds mainly on giant squid, grabbing its prey with teeth.

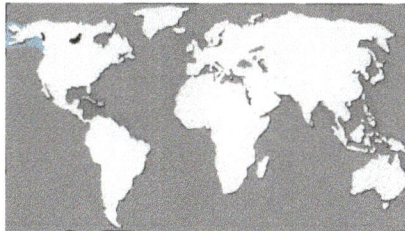

WALRUS *Odobenus rosmarus*

The walrus is a big animal. He's been known to use his tusks—which are no more than overgrown teeth—to pull himself out of the water.

Walruses may weigh as much as 2,000 pounds. They belong to a family of mammals called *Pinnepeds*. This family also includes Sea Lions and true seals. Because they eat meat, the walrus is a member of the order *Carnivora*.

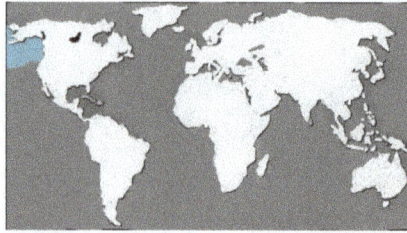

ORCA *Orcinus orca*

Orcas, also called killer whales, are the water wolves of the north. Members of the dolphin family, they are highly intelligent. People at a Sea World exhibit or other marine show are thrilled to see these huge mammals jump high in the air to grab a fish out of an attendant's hand. Orcas also work as a team. One recent National Geographic special showed a pack of whales working together to force a seal off a floe of ice and into the water so the orcas could attack it.

Orcas are the biggest members of the dolphin family, with distinctive black and white patches that readily identify them. They can reach lengths of 27 to 33 feet, and weigh 8,000 to 12,000 pounds. Orcas live in all of the world's oceans, and have even been known to enter *estuaries*. What are estuaries? They are bodies of water that flow into the sea, with rivers (fresh water) flowing into them. Usually, orcas don't stray very far from the ocean. In United States waters outside of Alaska, orcas have mostly been seen in the Pacific Ocean off the coasts of Washington and Oregon. However, orcas have also been spotted many miles from the ocean in the Columbia River, which separates Washington from Oregon.

Perhaps you've watched science fiction movies that show orcas remembering some human who did a bad deed to one of their *pack* members. (A pack of orcas is a group of them). The orcas somehow remember the person's boat and gang up to attack it next time the boat is on the ocean. It's not known if orcas carry grudges, but certainly not to the extent movies would have you believe. Or perhaps you've seen movies where dolphins can actually speak a few words of the English language. This is all greatly exaggerated. Dolphins don't have the working mouth parts to actually *enunciate*, or form, words of the English language. Still, dolphins are highly intelligent and have been taught maneuvers and tricks.

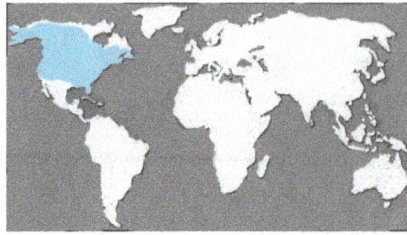

BALD EAGLE *Haleaeetus leucocephalus*

Our nation's symbol is the bald eagle. It is supposed to stand for courage, defiance, and strength. Benjamin Franklin, one of our Founding Fathers, wanted the wild turkey as our national symbol.

Franklin saw the eagle as "cowardly" because it sometimes stole prey from other raptors. However, he was outvoted by the other Founding Fathers. The eagle, however Franklin would have us believe, was simply stealing the prey to survive. He's merely found some shortcuts for getting what he wants. This is why the eagle is a survivor; he knows how to fulfill his needs. This is known as *adaptation* of the fittest.

At one time the bald eagle's numbers were greatly reduced by pesticides such as DDT. Since banning the use of DDT, the bald eagle has made a complete recovery.

In Alaska there is a subspecies of bald eagle that grows quite large. It is called the sea eagle, and feeds primarily on fish or fish remains. Alaska has large numbers of these birds, so many, in fact, that during the annual river runs of salmon, trees nearby will be covered with the eagles. They'll swoop in and devour the carcasses of dead salmon or pick off leftovers from bear kills.

SNOWY OWL *Nyctea scandiaca*

The main diet of the snowy owl is lemmings. However, they are opportunists, and in the harsh, bleak world of the northern *tundra,* (frozen arctic plain) will eat any kind of meat they can find. When lemmings are not available the bird will eat mice, as many as 7 - 12 per day to meet its food requirements. One snowy owl can eat as many as 1600 lemmings per year. Like most other owl species, they are *nocturnal,* or active at night. Snowy owls also feed on ptarmigan, geese, and ducks.

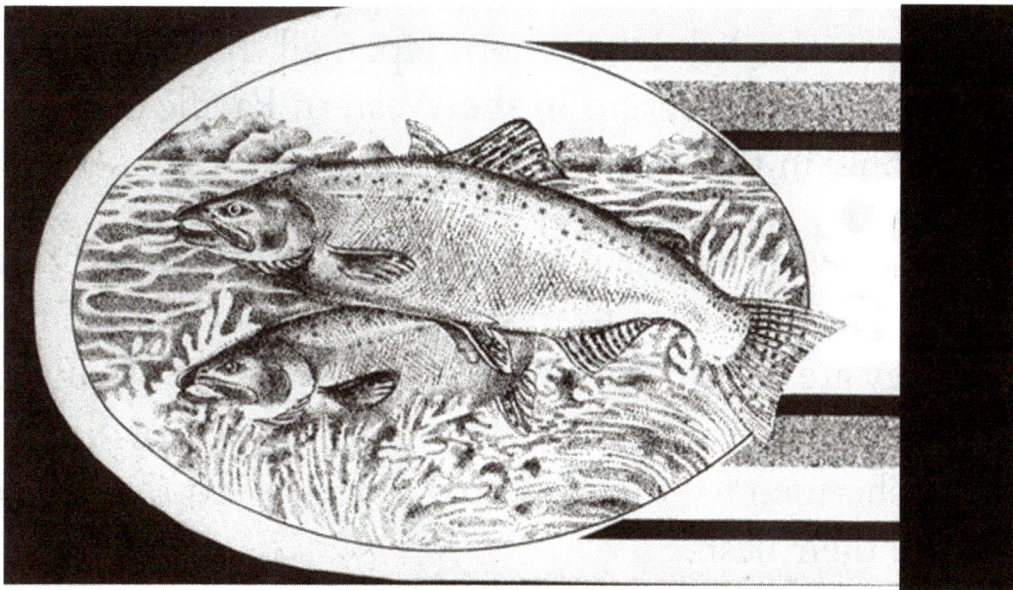

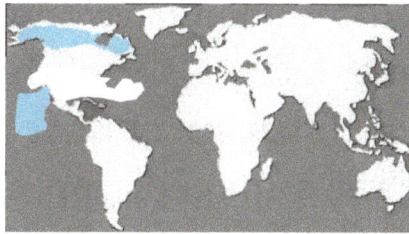

CHINOOK SALMON *Oncorhynchus tshawytscha*

Perhaps no journey has inspired more naturalists than the life cycle of the Pacific salmon. The salmon pictured above is the chinook salmon. This is our largest salmon, some males weighing upwards of 100 pounds. What amazes scientists (and continues to amaze) is how a salmon, after being gone from its birth waters into the ocean can find its way out of the sea and back up into the very area in fresh water where it was born.

Salmon are born in creeks and rivers. The very backyard creek that you go wading through might be a birthplace for a salmon. Chinook salmon are not just native to western North American waters. Salmon also live in northern Japan all the way north to Siberia. They are also present in the Western Pacific ocean, and China, but only in the Kamchatka peninsula.

Salmon migrate to the ocean and stay there from one to eight years. Some salmon return to fresh water earlier than their counterparts. They are referred to as *jack salmon*, and are usually smaller than a fish that has lived a full life cycle in the ocean. Salmon are prized by fishermen for their fighting abilities and the delicate flavor of the their flesh.

It is estimated that Pacific salmon have disappeared from about 40 percent of their former habitat. Overfishing, pollution in habitat streams, and other disturbances of their natural environment are all helping to make the salmon disappear. Juvenile salmon must have clean, undisturbed waters to live in. Chinook also need healthy ocean habitat. One sign of a healthy ocean is the presence of *algae*. Algae are green plants that can filter high levels of pollutants. Thus it is essential that algae are not destroyed in the oceans.

The rise of dams and hydroelectric power have also caused declines in salmon numbers, called salmon *stocks*. *Fish ladders* have been built for salmon to get around the dams, but aren't always successful. What is a fish ladder? It's a series of levels where water is flowing down, sort of like shelves of water. Salmon jump from one level to another, and in this way they get around the blockade of a dam. If you are lucky, maybe you've been to a dam and have seen the fish ladders and watched salmon jumping up or down them.

Chinook salmon have also been introduced into the Great Lakes to control the populations of alewives, small fish which were rapidly becoming a nuisance in the lakes. Coho (silver) salmon were also introduced, and the results were successful in controlling the alewives as well as providing sport for fishermen.

The species has also established itself in South America, where hatchery fish have escaped and established stable runs in local rivers and creeks.

Effect of climate on Arctic species

Global warming is hurting the walruses. There is a danger that they could dwindle to a fraction of their former populations. Recently, researchers in arctic waters found baby walruses alone without their mothers. If the baby walruses hadn't been rescued, they would have died. This has never before happened. Mother walruses are abandoning their calves because the sea ice is retreating and they need to stay up with the ice floes to find their food source: fish. The same fate is happening to polar bears. Each year, scientists study the thickness and amount of sea ice. They know the polar bear, for example, spends more time on the sea ice than he does on land. The ice is important for a bear to make its living preying on seals. Also, polar bears, who can swim sixty miles without tiring, are being found dead by drowning in the ocean, because they can't find enough ice to climb out of the water in time to rest. The larger gap between ice floes is also contributing to rougher seas, making the bear's swim more hazardous. The drowning of bears in the oceans is unprecendented; that is, it's never before happened like this.

In Hudson's Bay in Canada, for example, the ice-free time has increased by 20 days. This means less time for the bears to hunt, which is critical for their winter survival. Because of the decreased time to hunt, the bears weight has dropped, causing reproduction rates to decline, which means less bears.

The polar bear as the biggest bear in the world is a magnificent creature, and for its size and power deserves to be with us on this planet for all time.

One myth that some people seem to have is that the Arctic is a cold, distant place, devoid of almost all life. This is being challenged by studies today. This region is really a very sensitive area. What happens in the Arctic can affect our planet in ways we did not formerly understand. As the sea ice retreats and melts, bright surfaces are being replaced with areas not as exposed to sunlight. The result is storage of more heat...and the melting accelerates. This destructive cycle is *self-perpetuating*. This means it does not need outside influences to make it happen. In the year 2012, drastic changes in Arctic conditions were clearly noted.

There has long been concern over the release of *Greenhouse gases* that could be raising world temperatures. They are called Greenhouse because the result in the earth's atmosphere is like a nursery greenhouse; the gases cause permanent warming temperatures. This could be very destructive to habitats that have plants and animals that depend on the temperatures remaining cool.

It is fortunate for us, as a species that is dependent on other life cycles, that we now recognize how fragile our planet is, and how *interdependent* life forms are. Interdependence among living things means one life form needing something from another life form in order to exist. Plants and animals are interdependent; that is, they need something from each other in order to survive. Green plants give off oxygen which in turn is breathed in by animals. Animals give off, or exhale, carbon dioxide which is taken in by plants. Every living thing, or *organism,* needs something from some other organism. Even powerful animals such as the African lion are dependent on food sources such as the zebra and the African impala in order to ensure their survival.

Maybe you've watched butterflies flitting in your garden from flower to flower. What is the butterfly doing? It's looking for its food source, nectar. Without flowers, the butterfly would starve to death. In the same extent, the flowers are dependent on other insects such as bees. The bees pollinate, ensuring the survival of the flowers. These are more examples of interdependency.

These interdependencies scientists call the *Web of Life*. A web is like something that reaches out and interconnects with everything else. Everything moves around everything else, and has a direct or indirect effect on each other. Man, as a species is the only creature that has the thinking power and the capacity to upset the age old balance of the Web of Life on the planet.

Man, too, is part of the Web of Life. His technology has some-times removed him from living in harmony with nature, so it is up to him restore that balance.

Today, man has the capacity to use his wisdom and compassion to co-exist with the rest of the creatures on this planet. It cannot be left to the whim of a foolish few that some creatures on this planet are doomed to become extinct by man's hand; if we are to survive, our very survival depends on how we treat other living things on this planet.

Author Biography

Tom Romano was born in Eugene, Oregon. He grew up in Northern California, attending the California College of Arts and Crafts, Oakland, CA graduating with a B.A. in illustration. He got an A.A. degree in graphic design from the Art Institute of Seattle. He is currently pursuing a Masters degree. He is the author of two other childrens books, "Birds of Prey and Other Endangered Species," and "Jeweled Travelers of the Skies," as well as collaborations with other authors.

Mr. Romano currently resides in Portland, Oregon where he lives alone, but wishes for a cat to keep him company.

Acknowledgements

I wish to acknowledge my friend Ruth Wire and others in the Haywire Writers Group, Ashland, Oregon for their help in editing and helping make this book a realized dream.

I also wishes to thank my mother Ethel whose constant support through the years helped me to reach my goals.

Other Children's Books by Mr. Romano

Here are Mr. Romano's two other books that can be found on Amazon.com and through his other publisher, World Audience. com www.worldaudiencepublishers.com.

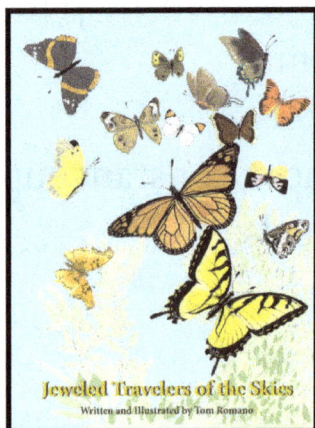

Jeweled Travelers of the Skies

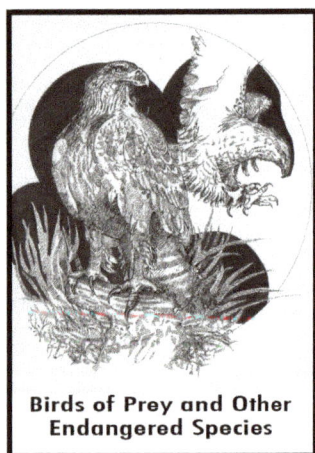

Birds of Prey and Other Endangered Species

Bibliography

1. Cheetahs by Dianne Macmillan, Lemer Publications Copyright 2009.

2. Big Cats (Wikijunior, wikibooks) wikipedia online

3. Ten Amazing Big Cats Online LISTVERSE by Hope September 13, 2008. http://listverse.com/2008/09/13/10-amazing-big-cats

4. National Geographic Society *Animal website* animals of the world.

5. World Wildlife Federation WWF Global. *Animals of ice and snow.*

6. Wildlife *Biomes of the Earth* National Geographic Explorer http://wesbiomes.weebly.com/tundra.html

Contacts for AB Film Publishing

Here are some websites to get in touch with the publisher:

1. www.abfilmpublishing9.wordpress.com

2. www.alanbaxter33.wordpress.com

3. abfilm@yahoo.com

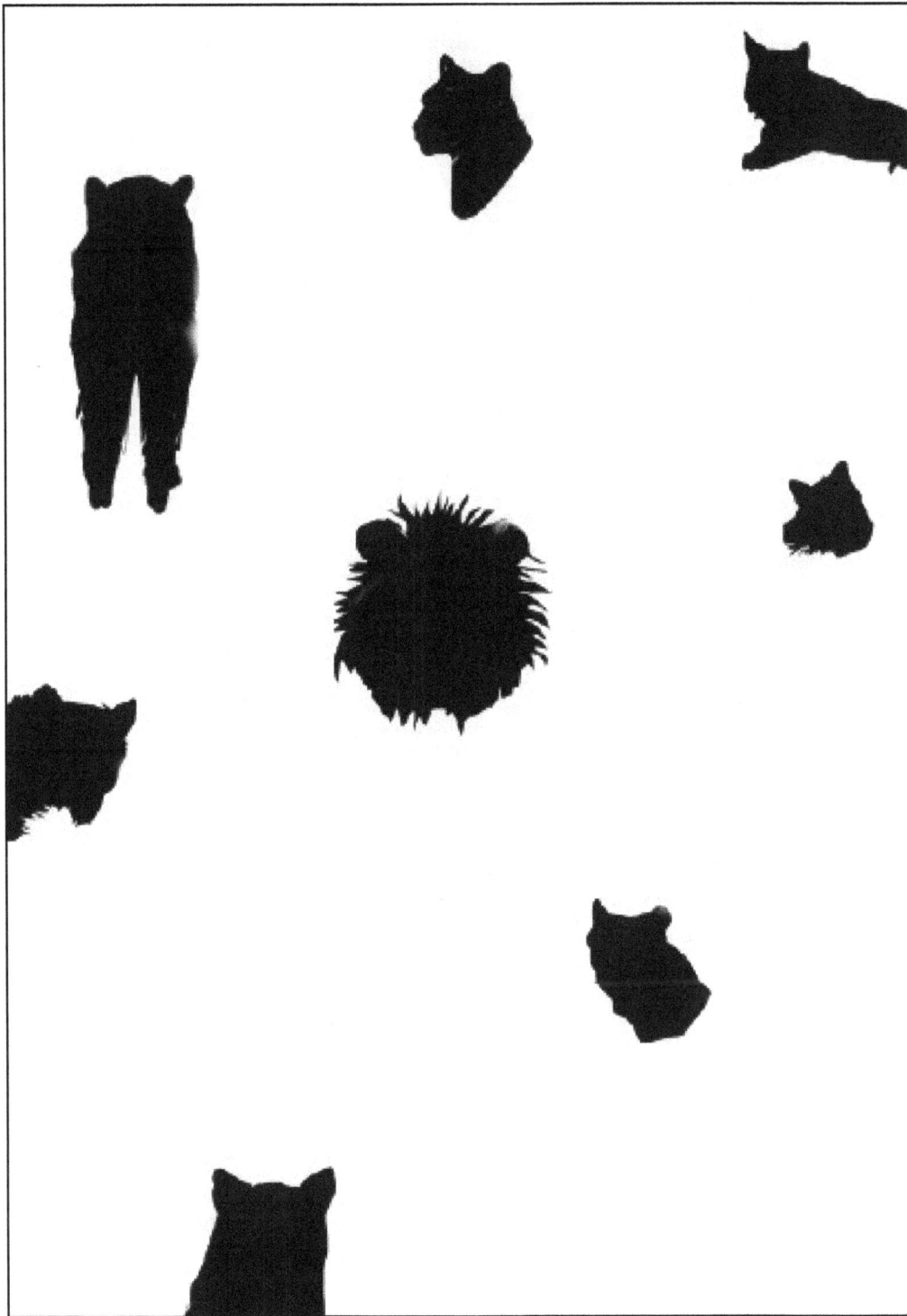

Can You Identify these members
of the feline family?

Wild Creatures
of the World

Written and Illustrated by Tom Romano

AB FILM PUBLISHING   www.abfilmpublishing9.wordpress.com

www.ingramcontent.com/pod-product-compliance
Lightning Source LLC
Chambersburg PA
CBHW081157090426
42736CB00017B/3364